THIS IS BASEBALL

GAME TODAY 1PM

TICKETS

BOX AND RESERVE

ALL SEATS

TICKETS

by Margaret Blackstone
pictures by John O'Brien

SCHOLASTIC INC.

New York   Toronto   London   Auckland   Sydney

For my father, Henry
my son, Dash
my husband, Tom
and my brothers, Pete and Neil
all great boys of summer
and for my friend, Elissa
one of the great girls of all seasons
—M.B.

For Tessie,
the first in my lineup
—J.O'B.

Text copyright © 1993 by Margaret Blackstone.
Illustrations copyright © 1993 by John O'Brien.
All rights reserved. Published by Scholastic Inc., 555 Broadway,
New York, NY 10012, by arrangement with Henry Holt and Company, Inc.
Printed in the U.S.A.
ISBN 0-590-48528-8

9 10 11 12   08   08 07 06

THIS IS BASEBALL

This is a stadium,

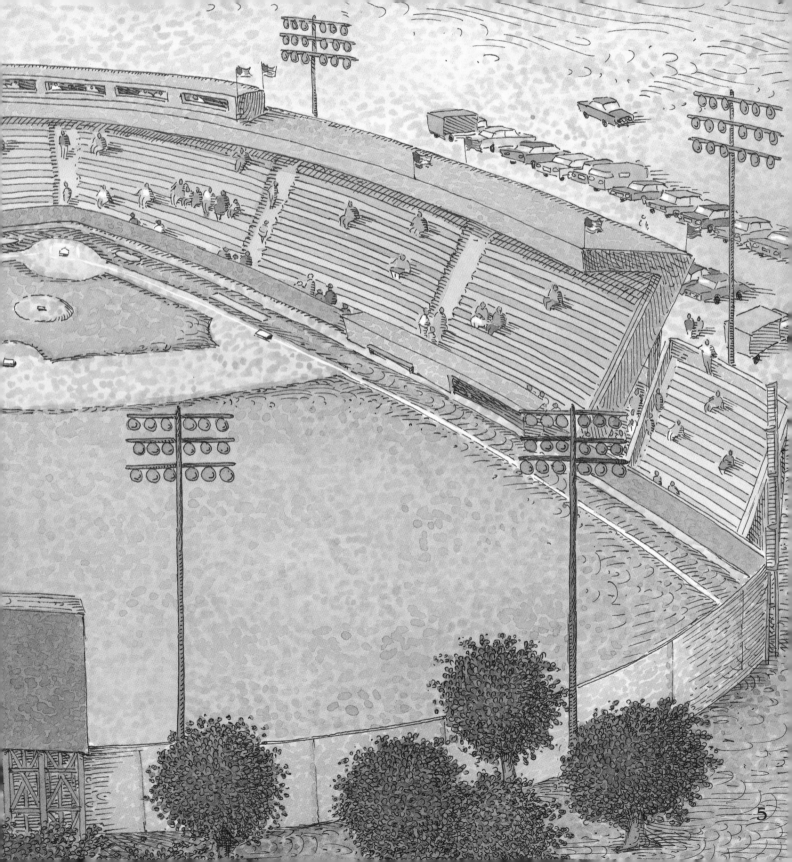

and this is a baseball diamond.

This is one team,

and this is the other.

These are the fans.

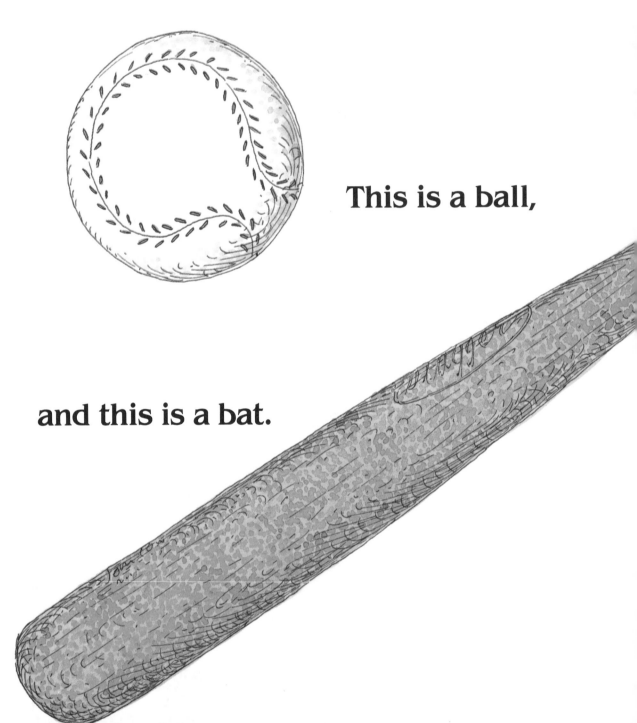

This is a ball,

and this is a bat.

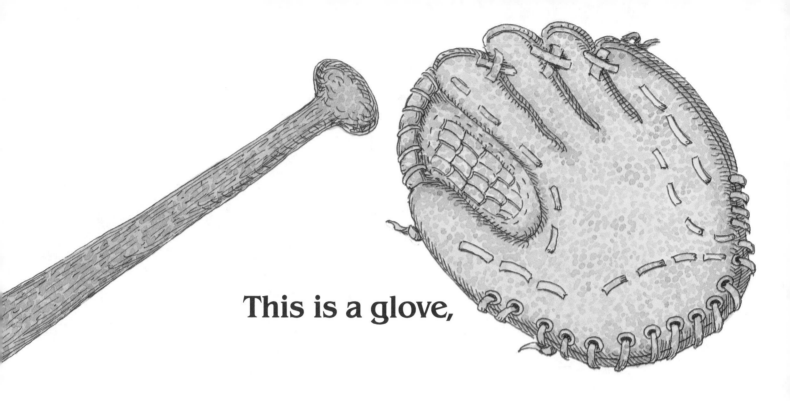

This is a glove,

and this is a cap.

This is a player.

And these are the umpires who call the game.

This is a pitcher.

This is a catcher.

This is the infield.

This is the outfield.

This is a pitch.

And this is a hit!

This is a high fly ball to deep left field...

and this is a
HOME RUN!

This team has won,

and this team has lost.

Tomorrow there will be another game.